I Can Make it Through the School Year *for Teachers*

POWERFUL LESSONS TO SURVIVE AND THRIVE

Crystal Byrd

All Scripture quotations, are taken from the Holy Bible, King James Version (Public Domain).

I CAN MAKE IT THROUGH THE SCHOOL YEAR FOR TEACHERS.
© 2017 Crystal Byrd.

All rights reserved. Printed in the United States of America. No part of this book may be used or reproduced in any manner whatsoever without written permission except in the case of brief quotations em-bodied in critical articles or reviews.

Cataloging-in-Publication Data is on file with the Library of Congress.

Byrd, Crystal.
I Can Make It Through the School Year for Teachers: Powerful Lessons to Survive and Thrive / Crystal Byrd
p. cm.
ISBN 978-0-9977722-0-3 (trade paper)
1. Spiritual life-Christianity. 2. Social Issues   3. Education.
I. Title

For more information visit
http://www.crystalbyrdbooks.com

Dedicated to teachers
everywhere whose hard work
makes education possible.

"That I may publish (proclaim)
with a voice of thanksgiving, and tell of all
thy wondorous works."
Psalm 26:7 (KJV)

CONTENTS

	Introduction	vii
1	Chapter 1: His Power, His Love	11
2	Chapter 2: His Divine Intervention	17
3	Chapter 3: His Presence	19
4	Chapter 4: His Plan for New Beginnings	21
5	Chapter 5: His Timing	27
6	Chapter 6: His Armor	31
7	Chapter 7: His Encouragement	35
8	Chapter 8: His Will	39
9	Chapter 9: His Voice	41
10	Chapter 10: His Results	43
11	Chapter 11: Ask and Pray that You Shall Receive	45
12	Chapter 12: The Pressure Culture	49
13	Chapter 13: Maintain Mode	53
14	Chapter 14: Isolation Woes	55
15	Chapter 15: Work Life Integration	59

16	Chapter 16: Burn Zone	63
17	Chapter 17: Managing the Big-S	67
	Creating a Stress Prevention/Reduction Plan	
	Identify the Problem	
	Identify Your Stress Triggers	
	Phases of Response	
	Responses to Stress	
18	Chapter 18: Management Techniques	77
19	Chapter 19: Determine Your Why	87
20	Chapter 20: Teachers Need Options	89
21	Chapter 21: Transitions	91
22	Chapter 22: Career Reflection	93
23	Chapter 23: Do What You Can	97
24	Chapter 24: Changes on the Horizon	99
25	Chapter 25: I Can and Will Make it Through the School Year	101
	Epilogue	105
	References	111

YOU CAN

(AN INTRODUCTION)

I can't, I can't, I can't make it through the school year, is a phrase that often resonates with teachers. Although we may not say it aloud, it is an internalized feeling. Working in a public service profession can be demanding, frustrating, and stressful. On the other hand, it can be rewarding, life changing, and a positive challenge.

One thing is sure, the job demands can drive teachers to live unhealthy lifestyles and carry heavy workloads. We put in long hours, lose sleep, and deal with immense amounts of pressure and stress from various aspects of the job. We begin to fizzle from the stress and break under the load. The absences begin to pile on. The dreadful morning we must return to work lurks in the front of our minds. We begin to look at everything that is wrong; it consumes us. We then fall prey to the circumstances and the situation/s that we find ourselves in. Never, in a thousand years, when we enter education do we think it will be this way. Yet, we end up pulling our hair out…what little is left from everyone else pulling, too.

We came into the profession to make a difference, to teach others to have a love of learning like we do! Then bam, a year hits in which you feel like you will not make it through. The year you are screaming inside, beating yourself up for choosing this profession, and looking for a job elsewhere. Expectations can be quickly dashed when you realize that being a teacher is not all you thought it would be. Teachers need ways to counteract the work hazards of teaching and this can be achieved by being mindful and proactive. According to the Alliance for Excellent Education (2010) and the Edna Bennett Pierce Prevention Research Center (2016) the field of teaching is in a crisis.

During my years of hardships in education, I became consumed day and night by the situations I faced on the job: the lack of resources, the pressure to perform, feeling ineffective, and predominant politics in the educational system. Not everyone has a similar experience. It is likely the minority who do not have at least one rough year. It may be all roses for some. I have not met many in education who lacked in the hardship department. Teachers need encouragement and stress relief on the job but often do not find it. But there are places to go for encouragement, especially when a difficult year rears its ugly face. The hardships do not have to defeat you. There is hope. You can make it through the school year!

In this book, encouragement is offered to spur you to remain strong in the face of opposition and overcome the frustrating times. We'll look at unique plans for coping, finding the good in tough situations, keeping focus in the right place, and encouraging one another. Additionally, we dive deep into finding healthy responses to stress, pinpointing steps to make teacher life a bit simpler, and much more to support you through the school year.

Like countless other teachers who have gone before you, each of us has a story to tell and battle scars to share. Part of my story is the way God gave me strength through his Word. He showed me "I can do all things through Christ which strengtheneth me" (Phil. 4:13). He opened doors that no man could shut and shut doors that no man could open (Isa. 22:22). God orchestrated situations for good even when it did not seem like he was listening. He was there ordering my steps, leading me in the right direction, and offering hope through the Bible and other people. He placed individuals in my path at the perfect moment to lift me up. He reminded me that we are not alone, and he is there through it all. He taught me about battles bigger than myself and how to overcome during difficult times through faith, obedience, and love. He gave me wisdom on how to approach each challenge I faced. What he did for me, he will do for you because he is not a respecter of persons (Rom. 2:11). We can stand strong and move forward through the strength and power God provides.

1

HIS POWER, HIS STRENGTH

Every day we walk into the school we face battles. It may be battles from your class, the office, the system, or all of them. One thing for sure is that the battle rages. When we enter teaching, we do not see the battles lurking around the corner, so naturally we are not proactive about the battles we encounter. In the Bible, David was tending to sheep and faced a lion and a bear. If I think of caring for sheep, a lion and a bear do not cross my mind. However, they did cross David's path and he had to respond accordingly. He was proactive and prepared for possible encounters. He had a plan to protect himself and the sheep. He knew he had God's power and strength to face each obstacle. We too, need God's strength and power to face ours.

My toughest school year started out hectic. Upon my return from summer break our school went from two special education teachers to one, *me*, and from several aides to *one aide*. Due to the recession and funding cuts, reduction in force was in place, eliminating jobs. During this period, I serviced the special education population from kindergarten to sixth grade, took over all the Local Education Agency (LEA) paperwork (which I was new at), and continued to uphold the responsibilities I had previously. My plate overflowed. It was the worst of worst years. Plus, I was a rookie teacher.

As the days progressed I dreaded going to work. Feelings of trepidation began to consume my daily life. I complained that the needs of the students could not be met realistically with one person doing this many jobs. Planning periods and paperwork preparation time were scarce. I stayed late at work and took work home to accomplish the mountain of tasks. Like many other teachers, I did my best to work in a difficult situation with limited support.

The troubles intensified and continued. It appalled me. How could I be put in such a bad situation with limited supports and training, and be looked upon with disdain? It perturbed me deeply. Most of all, I wanted what was best for the students, and I was willing to go to battle for them.

My first response was to figure out a way to make the situation better and resolve what I could. On high alert, I went to work on the situation.

Here is a mini list of things I did in my own strength/power:

- Ensured all stake holders were aware and involved
- Kept notes on everything
- Created a SMART plan to remediate my areas of weakness
- Searched for solutions online
- Researched new careers/jobs
- Created a plan for a possible job change

During this time, I often wondered about the rights of the teacher. Students had rights, parents had rights, but what about the teacher? What safeguards were in place for the teacher? The way I saw it there were not many, if any, to protect teachers. However, there are forms of protection through the state, if needed.

Across many districts it was a difficult time for several employees who found themselves in similar situations. These types of situations put people on pins and needles. We questioned who to trust, often remained silent, and information was rarely divulged with details of the struggle. Due to the nature of teaching, the circumstances in this book are spoken of in vague terms. I really am not able to paint the picture that is needed. However, I included enough information to provide some insight into the battle.

Difficult times as these call for rallying together with a prayer group to bring strength. I did not join a prayer group because of my own fear. This was a lonely period and it seemed like no one understood what I was truly going through. During this dark period, God brought to light that as humans we often do not let go of trying to solve our own problems and this leaves his hands tied. He revealed we need to let go or stop trying to solve it in our own strength and power in order to receive the divine intervention he has for our situation.

I took a day to pray and pour out my heart and frustrations to God. Shortly after I finished praying, a minister called from out of the blue and shared how God placed it on his heart to contact me. I am thankful for obedient, spirit-led people and God's divine intervention.

The minister shared the poem "Broken Dreams." This was the first time I had heard it. He conveyed we have to trust God and not try to handle life in our own power. I knew I had been fighting this battle within my own strength, and I was trying to correct all the work-related issues in my power to make the situations better. It was not working. Negative feelings and thoughts began to affect every relationship I had (i.e., marriage, children, extended family, and friends). I lived my life consumed by the circumstances. I permitted the hardships to weigh me down in every area of life. I learned the hard way on this one.

The actions I took in my own strength were best practice and I had a plan. However, my first course of action now is to take it to the Lord in prayer, and rely on the strength and power he supplies. We do not have control over the things that happen, but God does! We often try to solve problems on our own, or we run to others to help solve the problem/s. This is frequently the case in education. We face a problem and instead of giving it to God and trusting he will work it out, we attempt to work it out. Taking it to the Lord in prayer first could have saved me months of headaches and trouble. I share this experience and my heart so others can have a plan to take the problem or situation to God before making any decisions or taking any action. Listening for the still small voice speaking to your heart will lead you to the best approach to deal with your situation to avoid making similar mistakes.

As I faced dealing with difficult circumstances, co-workers who had their own battles, and continuing to do the job with limited support, I had to lean on God by allowing him to take control of the situation. I had to approach it in the spiritual realm and not the physical. I did what the Word said. First, I gave it to God and did not look at the circumstances. Then I trusted in God's promises that he would never leave me nor forsake me, that he would be my strength, and help me overcome.

I stood on God's Word. The Spirit led me to scriptures that spoke to my situation and I trusted in those words. I prayed, fasted, and overcame the situation by doing what is right. When I did it God's way, the Lord was able to take over and do what he had planned all along. The battle became the Lord's and not my own (2 Chron. 20:15). Look to God and not yourself for the solution/s. He will guide you through the situation and direct you on what you need to do in the battle. In his power, we can triumph in our battle because he goes before us each day into battle (1 Chron. 14:15).

I have stood on many passages throughout the school years. I will not be enduring much in my own power. My own power is weak and feeble. I rest on the power of the Word.

These verses are plastered in a frame next to my work station. A continuous reminder that I cannot do it alone.

"And he said unto me. <u>My grace is sufficient for thee</u>: for my strength is made perfect in weakness" (2 Cor. 12:9). "This is the day which the LORD has made; <u>we will rejoice and be glad in it</u>" (Ps. 118:24). "I can do all things <u>through Christ</u> which strengtheneth me" (Phil. 4:13).

Also, read the underlined sections together for a hidden message!

Despite the difficulties, all things are possible, and you can make it through the school year in the power and strength God provided by holding tight to the words of the Lord and keeping them before you. Remember he has plans to prosper you and he hears your heart's cry before a word has ever been spoken.

Reflect on a few questions to determine how you deal with difficult times.

- Are you facing a challenge today that you are trying to solve or deal with in your own strength and power?
- When faced with difficult circumstances or situations what is your first response?
- Have you surrendered every area of your life to the Lord?
- Are you trusting in the Lord and his Word to work out your situation?

2

HIS DIVINE INTERVENTION

I use to think prayer was some formal ritual. I thought you were supposed to get on your knees and be there long enough to at least require a pillow for cushion. I battled with this ideal and one day a friend dropped by my home to visit. Out of the blue she said, "What do you think prayer is?" Immediately, I knew it was the Lord speaking to me. I did not respond but she continued with wisdom. "It is talking to God and you can do it anywhere at any time."

It is not always on your knees; it can manifest driving down the road or walking around the school campus while you lift what is on your heart to the Lord. We often try to be strong and deal with our own stuff. God does not desire for us to carry the load. "Casting all your care upon him; for he careth for you" (1 Pet. 5:7) is the first step to divine intervention. Give him your frustrations and aggravations. He calls, "Come unto me, all ye that labour and are heavy laden, and I will give you rest" (Matt. 11:28). He wants you to rest at his feet and lay your burdens down. He will dry your tears (Rev. 21:4), impart peace into your life (John 14:27), and continue to be your refuge (Ps. 62:8). He is faithful and just to hear our cry and intercede for us.

Making prayer a part of your day will connect you to the divine. No matter where it happens, it just needs to happen. God hears our heart's cry and the prayers we lift to him. He will help us make it through each school day and before we know it we have made it through the school year. Teaching is not for the faint of heart. It is a tough job with demands beyond measure.

Request God's divine intervention by praying to the Lord. Abraham Lincoln put it best when he said, "I have been driven many times upon my knees by the overwhelming conviction that I had nowhere else to go." You can pray to God and talk with him when there is no one else to confide in or when you are at a loss of where to find solace. He is there waiting to hear from you. When we seek him with our whole heart we will find him (Jer. 29:13) and the presence of his divine intervention.

3

HIS PRESENCE

In the middle of a battle you can feel like the lone solider at war looking around for back up. However, you are not alone, and others can relate to your battle/s. They may not have experienced your exact hardship, but others have felt the same way you have at some point in life. Jesus felt like this at the cross as he hung in pain from being crucified (put to death by being nailed to a cross). He felt let down by many, even his heavenly Father. Shortly before his last earthly breath he asked, "My God, my God, why hast thou forsaken me?" (Matt. 27:46). God had not forsaken Jesus. God was there, and he is there in the midst of your battle standing for you and not against you. He is all around you. Trust that he is there like a great teacher, planning and implementing the plan. He is working out your situation, even when you cannot see it unfolding. He sees the bigger plan for your life. Keep your eyes on the Lord and see he is moving mountains for you. He is faithful!

One Wednesday evening after a long day of teaching, God came through for me. I stood in the prayer line at church, repeating to myself in thought, "I can't make it. I can't do this." The stress had taken me captive. I felt like an Israelite backed up against the Red Sea with Pharaoh and his army before me. Finally, my turn for prayer came. I stepped up and the preacher said, "You can and you will." I knew God was speaking to me. Only he could hear my thoughts and know what was on my heart. This gave me strength. It reminded me that God is with me and I am never alone. It is also the message I want to impart to you. You can and you will make it through the school year. Draw on the strength the Lord has to offer and the peace that surpasses all understanding (Phil 4:7) even in the very midst of your storm.

I believed the words God said, I just did not know how I was going to make it. God opened my Red Sea and parted it. God took me to the promised land, a place of new beginnings, by giving me hope and reassurance that he is there for me. "For I know the thoughts that I think toward you, saith the LORD, thoughts of peace, and not of evil, to give you an expected end (Jer. 29:11).

4

HIS PLAN FOR NEW BEGINNINGS

During one of my most difficult school years, each morning I awoke, the first thought of the day was today is a workday! Dread and misery immediately filled my heart. Partly from my own making and focusing on the wrong things. The Bible says to think on those things that are pure, lovely, and a good report (Phil. 4:8). At this point I was defeated. I was doing just the opposite of what the Word told me. Surely, there was something good I could think on, yet I did not. I got up thinking about the problems. I went through the day meditating on the situations. I complained to any soul who would listen. I went to bed dreading another day on the job. It began to affect my family, relationships, and who I was. The complaining was driving others from my life when I needed them most. I complained to my family the most about my frustrations and the dilemmas.

It is easy when you are stressed and frustrated to tend to vent to someone. This leads to constantly pondering on the problems and they become magnified. When I realized my response to this situation was part of my problem, I knew a change was needed. With prayer and a determined mind, I stopped complaining. I asked God to give me strength and to help me to find something good to think on. Proverbs 18:21 says, "Death and life are in the power of the tongue." The more I complained the longer I stayed in the same defeated place. I was defeating myself. I took a bad situation and made it even worse. I have termed this *dread mode*. Dread mode is a state of thinking and living based on the way an individual experiences feelings of dread and/or fear accompanied with anxiety related to a circumstance that is perceived or real.

Dread mode can be a time of personal growth. God can use this growth period to work things out in your life and reveal what is in your heart. This was true in my situation. Although it took me a while to get to this point. He made my heart more like his. He could only do this when I surrendered my thoughts of dread and bitterness about my circumstances to him.

God can turn anything around for good. He provided me a new beginning and he will provide one to you. If you have failed on the job, move past it, and start new today. There are steps you can take to start a new beginning toward a better school year.

Remember to pray first always. Recognize how you are feeling and responding in the situation. Are you turning to alcohol, withdrawing and becoming depressed, or maybe you are biting everyone's head off? Whatever your response, recognize it and determine if your response is the most effective way to handle your feelings. You may not be able to change the situation and you may not have control over it but, it does not have to have control over you. You have a choice on your specific response to the circumstance. Realizing your response will allow you to objectively look at what is working or not working for you at this present moment. The small foxes spoil the vine (Song of Sol. 2:15), so refuse to allow the little things of the day to steal your joy and dictate your attitude.

Create a new routine for each morning to start your day out right. It is a conscious choice. Start creating a plan the night before on how you will approach the new day upon waking. Open your eyes and speak with the Lord and thank him for all the good things in your life. You could access a Bible app on your phone and have it ready to read aloud to you while you get ready for work. You could leave yourself a message on the nightstand for the morning. It could simply read, "Smile, you have been blessed with another day!" It could be setting the alarm to go off with your favorite encouraging song. You may love humorous videos. Get the day going with a short humor filled clip. Post a scripture or saying that speaks to you or provides you strength or encouragement. Have a daily Bible verse or encouraging message sent to you via text message or email before you rise. Do what works for you. The key is to avoid repeating the same old things that do not work for your good. Find things to be grateful for in life. List them in a journal, on paper, or in notes on your device. Create the habit of focusing your attention on the good things each morning. Reread your list or make a new one. Just keep the good things before you.

Make a commitment to think and speak about positive things and resist complaining. "Resist the devil and he will flee from you" (James 4:7). This one can be tough because we are creatures of habit. Just continue to stick with it and you will see results. Avoid others who are negative and splurge with words. Have an escape plan from conversations that take a turn toward negativity. You could politely let them know you prefer to talk about uplifting topics because you are trying to be a more positive person, excuse yourself from the conversation, or speak wholesome words. You could say, "Excuse me, I must be going" and leave it at that. Redirect the conversation toward the positive. Refuse to be defeated by your own negative self-talk. Do not allow it to have its way. Find individuals to converse with who will lift you up and encourage you. Surround yourself with people who will motivate you to good and challenge you to become the best you can be each day. If you are not aligned with anyone at this time who possesses these qualities, the Word of God is a good place to start. He will lift you up and encourage you. "The word of God is quick, and powerful, and sharper than any two-edged sword" (Heb. 4:12).

Another way to look at this positive approach is the Pollyanna principle, which is based in finding something to be glad about no matter what circumstance or situation is before you. This is a practice to convert into a habit. If you live by this principle you are focusing on the good in a situation. It is all about how you look at it. There is truth in this principle.

In the account of the Israelites leaving Egypt to find their way to the Promised Land we see a perfect example of how perspective plays a pivotal role in outcomes. When twelve men went into the Promised Land to scope it out, ten men came back focused on the giants in the land, but two others saw something different. They saw a land flowing with blessings. When the day approached to go into the Promised Land the two men with favorable outlooks entered in and the others did not. (For the whole story, see Numbers 13.) Our perspective dictates how we respond and act in situations. Our thoughts are tied in with our attitudes and drive our actions and behaviors.

Around my most difficult school year I had a student teacher assigned to my class from a local university. We built rapport and I asked for her honest feedback about what I could change or what I could do better. She did not answer that reflective question at the moment. The next day, she arrived and we discussed the answer. So, what could I change or what could I do better? My attitude! My attitude was part stress, frustration, and disappointment that I had to stay in my difficult situation for so long without seeing any change. I allowed the situation to dictate how I acted, spoke, and responded to others.

In Acts 26, Paul and Silas were flogged, put in prison unjustly, and placed in chains. They were not the first people to be treated unfairly or to find themselves in a bad situation. Neither was I. However, my attitude was different. Paul and Silas sang praises to the Lord and prayed. Now I did pray and sing praise; however, it was not consistent at first. I allowed my praise to fizzle and my prayer to become ranting. When I finally entered *praise mode*, which is exalting the Lord despite circumstances, the chains in my life began to fall off and the prison doors were opened. My situation began to change when my attitude changed. I prayed about my attitude and praised God even when the situation looked bleak and change did not manifest. I lifted my hands and voice in adoration to the Lord when I did not feel like it. I thanked the Lord for the good and bad times. I did not have control over the situation, but I did have control over my attitude, prayer life, and praise life. God offers us new beginnings. Recognize where you are and how you are feeling and responding in the situation. Create a positive replacement behavior to the negative or unhealthy response. Lastly, make a commitment to this new beginning and in his timing, he will make all things beautiful (Eccles. 3:11).

5

HIS TIMIMG

Whose timing is better, yours or the Lord's? I arrived at work with complaints in my heart, feeling like that was not where I wanted to be or what I wanted to be doing. Overwhelm consumed me. I looked around at all the tasks before me and thought about how there was never enough time in the day to complete the tasks at hand. My soul cried out to have a more peaceful, reasonably manageable job. I scrounged for a hope to hold onto to make it through the workday. I wanted out of my frustrating job. I wanted God to bless me with a job that I had been patiently waiting for and to move me from the stressful domain that had occupied my work life. So I meditated (thought) on the word. "Trust in the LORD with all thine heart; and lean not unto thine own understanding. In all thy ways acknowledge him, and he shall direct thy paths" (Prov. 3:5-6).

I know in his timing he will bless me with a job that is beyond all that I can imagine, or he will equip me day by day to make it through the school year. He has done it before and he will do it again. However, I found myself feeling like an Israelite wandering in the desert. The Promised Land seemed so far out of reach. Yet, I did not want to be a complainer. I wanted to praise and rise to another level. I looked for the good in the situation and tried to fight the feelings that seemed to consume me. If I complain, I am sure to abide in *complain mode*. Complain mode is when an individual's focus is on the struggles in their life and they frequently complain about the circumstances or situations. They do not see a bright side of their dilemma, and they tell everyone they come in contact with about it.

The cycle of complaining is a hard habit to break. When you face struggles in the school setting there is a choice to be negative or resist the urge to fall into complain mode. If you are in complain mode, find things to be grateful for. Life for each person has a defined number of days to be lived. We want to live them with joy. Resist the urge to complain and look for the good.

"To everything there is a season, and a time to every purpose under the heaven" (Eccles. 3:1). I assume there is a season to complain. However, seasons should change and complaining should transition to a new season. God will move in your situation at the right time. He promises to put no more on us than we can humanly bear (1 Cor. 10:13). Things will begin to fall in place when he ordains it to be so. There are times to be still and patient, to wait on the Lord, keep his ways, and he shall exalt thee to inherit the land (Ps. 37:34). Listen for the prompting of the Holy Spirit to lead you or to reveal to you how to respond amid the storm. When we wait on the Lord we will be renewed and rise up out of the situation like the eagle in Isaiah 40:31. He will make a way of escape. This could be in the form of a new job or he may guide you in how to cope with the circumstances you face.

In waiting for God's prompting in my situation God directed my steps to be loving even when it was the opposite of what the world recommended. After being obedient to his instructions, peace infiltrated my life and it felt like God lifted a weight off me. Walking in love may manifest by you giving a gift, a smile, a kind word, or it may be going above and beyond. Do whatever the Lord prompts you to and you will find blessings.

Trusting in God is about keeping your focus on God, not on your feelings or the events before you. No matter what position in life you hold there will be some stress and battles. It is easy to want to take matters into your own hands and solve the problems you face. There is a natural tendency to find relief from the pain, whether it be physical, emotional, spiritual, or psychological. We want to alleviate suffering. God does not always answer in the timing and way we want. However, when he answers, he answers right. He works the situation and circumstances out for good (Rom. 8:28) while we trust in his timing.

6

HIS ARMOR

Are you familiar with the story of David and Goliath (see 1 Sam. 17)? Battles in education can seem like this. During the year that seemed to take me under, something peculiar happened. It was the end of another grueling school day. Many prayers were lifted from my heart to the Lord that day. As I sat at the kidney-shaped table many classes have, in walked two fourth graders. They brought me large stones, not rocks. They were a little smaller than the average size of a female fist. Each stone was smooth and clean. The children placed the large round stones from a northern lake on the table and said, "Here, Mrs. Byrd." I thanked them and they walked out. Instantly, the account of David and Goliath filled my thoughts. This was a gentle reminder that God would fight my battle if I put on his armor and not my own. David refused to put on the armor of man to face Goliath and he won the battle. He realized that the giant would not defeat him if he trusted in God. If we put on the armor of God, he will fight our battles too.

While in the heat of the battle, we tend to lose sight of the big picture. We want to win and bring the situation to a close. However, there are battles that are bigger than we are equipped to handle. Satan tried to intimidate me and put fear in my heart, but "greater is he that is in you [me], than he that is in the world" (1 John 4:4). Satan wanted me to be in a place of barely surviving and nowhere near thriving. He wanted to steal my joy and peace by using my job. When we face these types of battles, preparations to make the right choices are in order. I knew the Lord was speaking to me through those stones and he was going to help me defeat this giant in my life, just as David trusted the Lord to be faithful.

Your giant may be health related, a difficult home life, a complicated job, or anything that causes suffering. Like me, he will provide the armor you need to defeat the taunting giant lurking in your life. If you picked up this book, one of your giants is likely your job.

A good place to start preparing for battle is found in Ephesians 6:10-18. Putting this armor of God on will equip you for the daily battle you face on the job or in your personal life.

- Belt of Truth: Know the truth of God's word. Don't be deceived.
- Breastplate of Righteousness: Be a doer of what is right. Seek the Lord to help you be pleasing to him even when you do not feel like it.
- Gospel of Peace: Stand your ground and face the battle in peace. Share the gospel of peace.
- Shield of Faith: Believe God will do what his Word says. Live by faith, not by your sight.
- Helmet of Salvation: Trust in the salvation that is given through Jesus and not your own goodness.
- Sword of the Spirit/The Holy Bible: Read and meditate on the Bible. This is your weapon in the battle.
- Prayer: Pray always, for others and yourself, even your enemies.

Any battle you face is a spiritual battle. A battle of good versus evil. "For we wrestle not against flesh and blood, but against principalities, against powers, against the rulers of the darkness of this world, and against spiritual wickedness in high places" (Eph . 6:12).

Attacks from the enemy can manifest in different ways. If the principal sends an e-mail stating the whole staff is in subordination for not doing a weekly update on the school web page or a parent comes against you; you are in the battle. These battles are spiritual warfare. There are ways to address the attack of the enemy no matter the form of manifestation. Here is a short list on approaching the attack in the spirit and not the flesh:

- Pray
- Read the Word of God
- Rise above it, be bigger than the adversary
- Keep a smile on your face
- Focus on the good
- Recall God will turn it around, take you out of it, or provide you the strength to endure
- Do not rejoice in God's revenge. Pray for your enemies
- Keep God's ways (do the right thing) and remember God will take care of you

We each face battles in life, and during my battle the Lord led me to the book of Psalms. I read the chapters several times and confronted the attack in the spirit without observing any results. It was still months away, but God did just what he said he would do. He turned the situation around for good and delivered me from my giant.

7

HIS ENCOURAGEMENT

When a tough year comes you may long for some encouragement. We all need it. There are times it seems no one understands what we are going through and therefore they cannot encourage us, or they need encouragement as much as we do. When these moments arrive we can encourage ourselves, like David, when he encouraged himself in the Lord during his battle (1 Sam. 30:6). David was distressed in battle and everyone around him too. I don't know exactly what he was thinking the day he arrived and found life in ruins. I do know how he was feeling. He felt oppressed and defeated.

During my year of oppression, I visited a nearby church during a revival. The preacher announced the altar call and I went to the altar to be encouraged, lifted in prayer, and to get an answer to my dilemma. The preacher told me to praise the Lord through the battle even when you do not feel like it. Up to this point I had only complained. My praise was gone. One of my passions was singing and praising the Lord, but that had vanished from my life. That evening in faith I lifted my voice, thanking God for working it all out and for who he was. I ran around the church with a few others in faith that God had already worked out the situations at work. I did not feel like doing it. I felt the opposite. The moment I moved in faith I gained victory. That oppressive spirit lifted off me. I learned to walk in new found victory and you can too.

So what did David do to encourage himself? He put on the garment of praise for a spirit of heaviness (Isa. 61:3) by singing praises. Praise lifts the heart and focuses the attention toward God. If you feel oppressed, lift your voice toward heaven with thanksgiving. Speak the words out loud and proud in faith, "Thank you, Lord, for making a way!" Sing a praise from the bottom of your heart as if you already have victory over this heaviness. There are plenty of praise songs online that can be accessed in seconds. You can create your own from the heart. Keep lifting your voice in praise and adoration until the oppressive yoke breaks. Continually seek him and in due season you shall reap a harvest (Gal. 6:9). You can also encourage yourself by remembering God's promises to you.

He promises to:

- Never forsake you. (Deut. 31:6)
- Give you peace. (Prov. 1:33)
- Go before you into battle. (Deut. 1:30)
- Supply every need. (Phil. 4:19)
- Provide strength and power. (Isa. 40:29-31)
- Provide good plans for you. (Jer. 29:11)

Another way to receive encouragement is to give it. Be about the business of building up each other (1 Thess. 5:11). The job of educating is dynamic in nature. Supportive words can make a difference. Unconstructive feedback will likely tear down. This feedback could come in the form of negative talk from any stakeholder in education. How we manage our emotions will impact those around us. If we are harsh and demeaning, we compound the problems that exist in a conflicted system. Communication styles in education are diverse and we start with relating through our own style. If we make a positive or constructive comment daily the process has begun. As educators, we do have some control and step one is focusing on the things we can control. Think about the butterfly effect. Small consistent actions can compound to result in profound effects. In 1 Timothy 6:3, Paul states to speak wholesome words. Sharing a quote or Bible verse that has impacted your life can be an encouragement. Find something good to share. Give encouragement freely and you will be lifted up with a spirit of happiness and joy. This all begins with lining up with his will for our life.

8

HIS WILL

The Lord's will for each of us is to keep our focus in the right place. Public service work entails working with many personality types, including difficult ones. These individuals can be co-workers, parents, students, and those in authority over us. When frustrations arise from working with difficult personality types, our focus can be diverted. The negative feelings that arise are a tool the enemy uses to get our focus off God. It is a seed the enemy tries to plant in our heart. When we recognize that we have feelings of frustration we need to stop and pray. Pray for those who we are frustrated with and for God to help us deal lovingly with that individual or individuals. This breaks the yoke the devil wants to wrap around your neck to weigh you down. When we are weighed down we can't be as effective or get the job done in the same fashion as when the yoke is not there. Do not beat yourself up over this. Ask God to forgive you and move forward. Plus, it is not fair to the others we work with to let ourselves get to a place where our focus becomes diverted from teaching and making a positive difference.

In the school setting we have to be cautious to not focus our energy on having ill feelings toward anyone. At times, they have no more control over the situation than we hope to have. God's will is for our focus to remain on the good and be the best teacher for each student, even when it is difficult. We change what we can and acknowledge what we can't. When we have reached the end of our rope, God is there to do all that we could never imagine doing. He is there to lift you up and remind you that you can make it through the school day and the school year. When stress and frustrations build, the wrong attitude can arise; however, his grace is sufficient, and our strength is made perfect in weakness (2 Cor. 12:9). His will is easily fulfilled when we listen for his voice.

It is important to respond with biblical foundational principles to difficult personality types. There are some simple steps to divert the difficult spirit; remain humble, respond in love, and offer understanding. Try to understand the other person and see them through the eyes of God. His ways are higher than our ways. Extend the grace you would like to have and be the light that shines in a world so dark and dim.

9

HIS VOICE

What can you do when you feel overwhelmed by the pressures placed upon you, when you want to cry, or when you feel like screaming at the top of your lungs in distress? I had arrived at that day, faint hearted and bearing a heavy load. I wanted to say, I QUIT, and walk out. Opposition stared me right in the face, and I felt like I had to achieve the impossible. I thought I am one person and can only do so much. I went into the teacher's mail room and called my husband in private. I told him about the opposition and how I wanted to quit. I was so frustrated and felt beat down. Once I got off the phone with him, I asked the Lord, What should I do? I wanted to hear, leave and don't look back. Yet, the quiet whisper spoken to my heart was *stay and pray*. It kept ringing over and over in my heart. That is just what I did. In the end it paid off. God turned the situation around. It is a testimony of what the Lord can do when we listen to him and heed that still small voice that leads us down paths of righteousness. In listening to his voice, we receive the best results.

10

HIS RESULTS

In John 2, a truth is shared about how to get the best out of life. In the story of the wedding where the wine ran out, Jesus was a guest. The servants at the wedding sought out a solution from Mary, Jesus' mother. Mary went to Jesus to ask for his help. Jesus honored the request and the wine was better than the man-made wine. Mary informed the servants who sought a solution to the problem to do whatever Jesus told them to. Our problems are the same way. When struggling and needing a remedy, go to God. His solution will turn out better than any human approach. God knows what to do and when to do it. Submit your request in all things unto the Lord (Phil. 4:6) and "taste and see that the LORD is good" (Ps. 34:8). Trust him to lead you in the right direction and to "supply all your need according to his riches in glory by Christ Jesus" (Phil. 4:19).

Another lesson I learned through the hardships was to see situations through another's perspective. Supervisors have difficult jobs and many responsibilities, too. The Lord helped me to see the heavy administrative job responsibilities and their need for encouragement. We hope to have administrative support in the school where we work. However, this is not always the case. In these instances, do as the Word says and "whatsoever ye would that men should do to you, do ye even so to them" (Matt. 7:12). This requires strength and not our own strength. It takes the strength of the Lord. God rewards us for doing right and he will reward openly (Matt. 6:6). Go to the Lord in prayer for administration, even if this is a source of frustration, and watch the Lord work. If you listen for the Lord, he will lead you to do good to others. Doing this will change the whole atmosphere. Let us not be weary in well doing: for in due season we shall reap, if we faint not. (Gal. 6:9). The results of the seeds you sow from prayer and an upright heart are in the Lord's hands. His results will always be better than our own.

11

ASK AND PRAY THAT YOU SHALL RECEIVE

The National Center for Teacher Statistics reports education has a turnover rate of 8 percent leaving the profession, 8 percent moving to new schools, and about 84 percent staying at the same school in the profession (Goldring, Taie, & Riddles, 2014). However, for teachers who have been in the profession for one to five years, the average that leave teaching is about 27 percent based on data from 2008–2012 (Gray & Taie, 2015). Attrition of teachers is a concern and continues to be a concern for the profession. There are several good reasons why educators leave the profession. Having pondered leaving the profession, I can attest to this.

Many times, personnel support is not available or deemed as one of the most important investments. New trends in turnover rates in education could emerge due to lack of supports.

I had the opportunity to work with a first-year special education teacher and LEA at her assigned school. At the end of the year, she shared that she could not do this her whole life, therefore she went back to college to obtain a different degree. During her tough year, she received a memorandum for doing what she thought was best at the time. However, administration did not agree that her choice was best practice and she was reprimanded. These instances are common. Dealing with difficult situations with little support is another reason great teachers leave (Hughes & O'Reilly, 2015).

Many stay in education due to financial obligations and some stay because they fear change. The reasons for staying are various. Teachers stay out of obligation or for the benefits. Some stay because they are on a mission to make a difference. There are positive and negative reasons to the decision to go or stay. The reasons for leaving are a mile long. The predominant messages that resonate are I am trying to hold onto retirement, and I have to find a new career. These can result in less than a whole-hearted effort to educate and be present in the moment. We are educating the future leaders and problem solvers. Importance is high for providing the tools, personnel, and support systems to drive teacher effectiveness.

It should not be a crime to ask for what you need. However, in some school cultures or school districts, you could be treated poorly for seeking additional resources to effectively do the job. Especially, if larger amounts of money are involved. For example, a student with severe needs enrolls in your school and needs an aide. The parent is uneducated about what their child should be provided to meet the needs. Therefore, they do not request an aide or the parent refuses to allow the student to receive support from an aide. The teacher is expected to change a child's diaper and manage irate behaviors while still instructing a classroom. In either case support is needed. This would likely come in the form of an aide. However, in both cases an aide was not assigned until the teacher asked and pushed for the support he/she needed, even if he/she had to go to other outside agencies to get the support the student needed.

We should be able to ask for support for the students and the request at least be considered and hopefully honored. If you find yourself facing unsupportive administration, you can start at the feet of Jesus. Do not be weary in well doing for in due season you shall reap a harvest (Gal. 6:9). Teaching is a ministry and we can become weary.

Ward off the weariness by laying down your burdens at Jesus feet.

1. Tell God how you are feeling.
2. Ask for his guidance and strength.
3. Seek the Lord's guidance, wisdom, and strength through prayer and reading the Bible.
4. Ask others to pray for you and wait on the Lord.

He knows our every need and the students' needs. We often have not because we ask not (James 4:2). Sometimes we have to ask the Lord above and then make our request known to those in the position to provide the needed supports.

When you address an issue, you could be rocking the boat. You will need wisdom in addressing the issue. Laying low can buy you time, but it will not make the problem/s go away. God will lead you to know the right timing to address any issue. During periods of waiting, God is behind the scenes working. Keep pressing toward the mark even if the pressure mounts.

12

THE PRESSURE CULTURE

There are innumerable pressures that come with the job. As educators we must manage the culture of the educational system, the school system, the school we work in, and the community. These pressures come in many forms and because we do not visually see culture at a glance, it is a factor that can be overlooked. Culture is partly based on beliefs and attitudes.

Here are some pressures you may find yourself facing daily:

- Pressure for students to perform, even if they are slow learners.
- Pressure to get it all done and done now.
- Pressure to use your own resources to purchase supplies, printing, and attend professional development.
- Pressure from some parents to make sure their child gets good grades. Note: I did not say pressure to make sure they are learning and growing.
- Pressure to get in hours of teaching time when the day has several disruptions.
- Pressure to get a student who is absent caught up in a timely manner and still continue to move forward with the other lessons.

- Pressure to do your own interventions to ensure that students are progressing, yet with inadequate time to effectively provide interventions.
- Pressure from a lack of personnel to provide the services needed for special needs students and to implement programs.
- Pressure to be an outstanding teacher and for students to perform on mandated state test.
- Pressure to pay attention to details to avoid disparity (e.g., attendance, paperwork, racial and special population compositions, student-teacher ratio, etc.).

The list continues. All educators are keenly aware this list is not exhaustive and the depth of the strain is more than any word can describe. Handling the pressures can be exhausting. Pressures can turn to stress and stress to burnout. The goal is to prevent the stress from compounding and taking over your life by being proactive.

Let's address an approach to a few pressures. One of my pressures was for students to perform, even if they were slow learners. I resolved to do my best to teach the students and knowing that I did my best was enough. Another pressure was trying to get it all done now. I learned to determine what had to be done this minute, this hour, this day, and this week. Some things on my list could even be removed or put on the complete later list. This type of system enabled me to put the tasks into perspective and accomplish more of the important tasks at hand. Delegating can be your best friend, too. One school I worked in had frequent activities on a regular basis. This caused the teaching block to be interrupted often. When the yearly survey came out and the question arose, "What can we do better?" We suggested activities be grouped together. This would keep more days open for teaching and less days disrupted. The next year, the school tried the recommendation and from the teacher perspective it worked beautifully. The point is to be open and honest about the pressures and, with the right attitude, offer true solutions to any pressures you encounter.

What pressures are you dealing with now? Determine those pressure points and identify the pressures you can change. Select one or two to begin working on today. List out several ideas or ways to approach the pressure point/s effectively. When you have dealt with one pressure point move onto the next in a similar fashion and try to resolve or alleviate what is in your power.

13

MAINTAIN MODE

There comes a time in education when maintaining is the only option. This is *maintain mode*. Maintain mode signifies daily, sometimes hourly, survival. This entails maintaining the daily teaching schedule and handling the immediate things to be done. Growth outwardly is limited when in maintain mode. Inward growth continues to occur and will take time to manifest outward during these periods.

Times that signify maintain mode:

- New to the profession
- Too many changes at once
- Personal job change in education
- Curriculum changes
- Implementing new programs
- Administrative changes or management style changes
- Life crises (i.e., death in family, poor health, family member ill, and so on)

Know you will likely encounter a time and season in which you will solely maintain. When this time frame presents itself, accept that it has arrived and recall that transition periods pass or come to an end.

Are you in a time of transition on the job? If so, what transition are you experiencing? How long do you project it will take to adjust to the transition? (Note: It is difficult to determine a time frame for adjustments to life crisis experiences. Therefore, projected calculations related to life crisis are not necessary.) Calculating the time frame can provide perspective and bring realization that your situation will not last forever, because joy will come in the morning (Ps. 30:5).

14

ISOLATION WOES

Isolation can occur quickly in education. Being a teacher is a complex and demanding job. Mentors are assigned to teachers, and mentors are busy handling the duties and responsibilities of their own job assignment. This can result in a minimal to non-existent mentor relationship. Teachers are pressured to seek answers from the internet and others after work hours. This is time consuming and frustrating. Not all sources are reliable or relevant and the information varies over districts, states, and countries.

It is hard to relate to others who have not served in the same capacity in education in regards to individual educational concerns and issues. The magnitude of the job and the intricacies are complex. It is pertinent that we have experienced individuals to converse with about the educational challenges we face, without placing extra burdens on the shoulders of others that are carrying the same load and often heavier loads. This is another challenge in itself. This can lead to extra stress, burnout, and wasted money. To resolve challenges we share our frustrations with others and sometimes anyone who will listen. Many teachers complain about students with behaviors and about the profession as a whole. This complaining can add to the feeling of isolation because others may disengage from interactions when complaining begins. This causes the cycle of frustration to continue unless we resist the urge and break the pattern. It can also attract other like-minded complainers and the cycle of complaining deepens and can seep into other areas of your life.

    Choosing wisely when and where to complain is key. On one hand, we all need someone to share our frustrations with. On the other hand, we do not want to be sucked into a vat that will pull us further away from positive influencers. Selective complaining is the middle ground. Complain when it is necessary and not about every little thing under the sun. Choosing wisely when to complain, where to complain, and whom to complain to can head off problems. Avoid public complaining, which could lead to the hot seat. While in a restaurant, one teacher complained about a special needs student to a friend. Someone over heard the conversation and knew the family of the child in reference. A lawsuit came out of the situation and the outcome was not favorable. Selective complaining will help you remain focused on being positive and could save you tons of trouble including in your personal life.

Take inventory and be mindful of the times throughout a work day in which you complain.

- Are you an optimist (positive) or pessimist (negative)?
- Does your communication style tend to be complaining?
- How often do you complain?
  Always, frequently, occasionally, or never.
- How much of your conversations and your thinking are complaining?
  Very little, occasional, frequently, or continually.

Do you feel isolated from others in education or feel alone in the profession? If so, what reasons do you attribute to the isolation? Is it that you are an introvert and stay to yourself? Is it because you complain often and others avoid you? What is the cause? Pinpoint the root cause. Next, start taking steps to become more connected to others in the profession. Join a teacher Facebook group, teacher life group in your community, or create a group.

15

WORK LIFE INTEGRATION

The work of a teacher to plan, grade or mark papers, and find resources to instruct students takes enormous amounts of time. The time at school is never enough. Therefore, work is taken home to be done and this adds up to time invested weekly. Even the most effective teachers have done work at home. This compounded time enables you to do the job better and teach more effectively. However, it begins to eat away at the work life balance. According to the American Institute of Stress when stress levels become elevated, it can be difficult to connect, and communication is affected. Your family and marriage end up taking a back seat. The job consumes your free time and keeps you so busy you do not have bonding time with your spouse, children, extended family, or friends. Oh yeah, don't forget yourself. Being stressed and tired from excessive work causes major strains. Anything that was a pleasure becomes a chore.

Problems begin to compile. Problems at work are brought home and this causes more stress, which in turn goes back to work. The cycle continues. Each work day is spent working with children, then you go home, and it is hard to be 100 percent present for your family. You need a brain break, a moment to hear something called quiet. Your work life integration will depend on your season in life. Integrating work and life is possible and will take assessing where you are in life, determining what activities are essential and which ones can go. A fervent approach is needed to find the best way for you to cope with job-related tasks and still remain available mentally and physically for your family and yourself.

Answering a few questions will start the journey to integrating work and life beautifully.

- How well are you integrating work and life? Well, somewhat well, or not so well.
- What activities on a weekly basis do you participate in? (e.g., ball games, church functions, running errands, and so on.) Take inventory of these activities.
- How often do you participate and how much time do you dedicate to these activities? Which ones are a necessity and which ones can you eliminate?

Some things may need to be eliminated permanently and some temporarily until you are in a different season of life that allows more time to devote to the activity.

The goal is to have a balance in your work life that will provide time for yourself, some enjoyment, and time for loved ones. Life cannot be all about work for long durations or you begin to experience a lack of fulfillment.

There are several effects an unbalanced lifestyle brings. Integrating work and life can feel like a juggling act, especially during busy seasons of life.

Here are some downfalls of a life without a healthy integration:

- Strain on marriage: disconnection, lack of intimacy, little energy left to devote to the marriage
- Consumes free time: you can become so busy you do not have bonding time with loved ones

- Compiling problems: Each problem has a cause and effect. (Ex: You take work home, you take time away from your personal life.)
- Parenting: You exhaust your human resources at work and have very little to give to your own children at the end of the day.
- Self: You find it hard to meet your own needs (e.g., physical, spiritual, mental, emotional, etc.) or enjoy your hobbies.
- Do you recognize any area/s your life is out of balance? If so, in which areas and how? Identify what specific actions you can take to create more balance in your life. Can you find ways to complete the majority of your work within the school hours without taking time from teaching the class?

My life became unbalanced. Grading consumed a lot of time at home, as well as finding lessons/activities for the students. One way I handle grading now is to complete the grading as each test is turned in or use programs that make grading easier. This allows me to ask any clarifying questions about test answers and to provide immediate feedback on student progress. Currently, I only take writings home to mark up. I pay a few dollars each year to sign up with a couple of sites to easily access lessons and activities. The few dollars are well worth the time I obtain in exchange. This frees me at home to spend time with my spouse and children. Making simple changes adds up to avoid the burn zone.

16

BURN ZONE

I entered the burn zone. I asked the Lord numerous days to help me make it through the school year…I am burned out! I used the Pollyanna Principle and looked for other opportunities. I lifted up prayers, hoped, and pursued other vocational avenues. Yet, still struggled to make it through the school year. The research on getting burned out as a teacher is evident (Blaze & MDCPS, 2010) and ABC News reports teaching is one of the top most stressful jobs.

We were approaching the end of the school year, yet not close enough to close the year out. The students were anxious with state testing approaching and the rest of us were stressed trying to squeeze the workload in while every disruption imaginable interrupted the flow of the day. Yet, the goal is to keep moving forward and making progress even if the burnout seems to become magnified. What can an educator do in this situation?

First, we can pray for strength and pray for our co-workers' strength too. We are all in this together. Our common goal is to educate children while making a positive lasting effect on their lives. This vision often becomes blurred by the lesson plans, the meetings, the new shifts, and so on. We barely have time to think, much less remember why we do what we do!

Second, build in time for yourself and reflection time about what you spend a majority of the week doing…TEACHING! We need to remember why we do what we do and refresh ourselves in order to give our best to the students entrusted to us to teach and enrich their lives.

"Where there is no vision, the people perish". (Prov. 29:18). Keep the vision of making a difference in others' lives. When Martin Luther King said, "I have a dream," he was talking about the vision he had. Think of your vision and talk with others about it. It is easy to focus on the negative and lose sight of the vision you once had. One day someone said in passing, "We need new young teachers in the profession." They might have said this because older teachers tend to lose sight of the vision and become indifferent and complacent more often than a teacher fresh out of college. However, give that teacher a few years and the sizzle will begin to diminish. The load will become heavy and the teacher will begin to see the job has a lot more to it than meets the eye.

When I was a new teacher, I was naive. I thought, summers off, all holidays off, we only work from 8 to 3. Wow, what a job! Many don't see the planning and extra duties that come with the job, the one-to-two-times-a-school-day restroom break, or the lunches with twenty to thirty kids. We only see what the eye can behold, until we reach the position of teacher. Then things begin to change.

The load can be dealt with in many ways. One thing is for sure, we cannot carry the load alone. The Lord will help you carry the load by "casting all your care upon him; for he careth for you" (1 Pet. 5:7). We do not have to carry it alone. We can rely on the Lord to help us through the difficult times in teaching and life. We can make it through the school year with him by our side. We can also encourage others and seek out others who will encourage us. We can draw strength from each other and help build each other up. Satan wants to divide and conquer by causing confusion and trouble between people. He may try it on the job, the church, or the home. Whichever avenue he chooses, his goal is to separate. He wants you to be in the wilderness alone or at least make you think you're alone. This tactic allows him to prey on your weaknesses and to overcome you in your situation. Bind together with others in Christ. Two can withstand and threefold chords are not easily broken (Eccles. 4:12). You can stand stronger together in the Lord.

Do you have a personal vision or the school vision that is meaningful to you? If so, what is your vision? If not, what is a vision that allows you to add value to others and to reap delight in fulfilling? What picture do you want to paint daily until the masterpiece is finished?

When you race toward the burn zone it is easy to become unfocused and lose determination. Keeping the bigger picture in the forefront will assist you during times of burnout. We are here to serve. The classroom is our ministry ground. The school campus is where our lights shine through our actions, behaviors, and responses to the difficult circumstances we face each day. Even when we fall short we can get back up (Prov. 24:16). Your vision can draw you out of the burn zone.

Now comes the time to ask yourself where you are at and where you want to go.

- Do you want to continue to live and work in the same mental and emotional place you are now?
- What areas of life are affected at this time?
- If you are burned out, how is it affecting you?
- Are you in maintain mode, barely hanging on?
- Are you feeling isolated and alone in this battle?
- What pressures are you feeling and how are you coping with them?
- Are your coping mechanisms positive or negative in nature?
- Have you been carrying this load alone?
- Have you given your struggle to the Lord?

Examining where you are will assist in creating a personal plan to lead you to your desired destination on this teaching journey.

17

MANAGING THE BIG "S"-STRESS

Stress. We all have it and are aware that good and bad stress exists. This feeling of too many overwhelming pressures in life can leave an individual frazzled, perplexed, and drained. Learning to manage stress will keep stress from managing you and your peace can remain. It can be difficult to find the right balance in life from juggling the job to taking care of your own basic needs. Almost half of all teachers experience extreme daily stress. A majority of stressors in education are external in nature. (Greenberg, Brown & Abenavoli, 2016). Stress has a compounding effect, and thinking on the stress can add more stress to your life. Part of stress is worry. We tend to worry about things we have no control over, and these thoughts can take over our lives. Knowing your stress triggers and responses will help to alleviate stress and combat it. We will take a deeper look into stress to understand how we interact with stress in our daily lives and create a plan to reduce or prevent stress.

Creating a Stress Prevention/Reduction Plan

Without a plan it is hard to know what actions to take and what works for you. When an individual gets serious about reducing stress, their stress will be seriously reduced. Grab a device or paper and pen to record some thoughts and actions for your plan as we walk through some management skills and tips to add to your prevention/reduction plan. This plan is key to reducing the effects of stress in your life. Each individual's stress prevention and reduction plan will be unique according to what works for each person.

Identify the Problem

After contemplating the previous questions in the book, you can take the next step and think about the stressors in your life.

What causes your stress and what are the sources of frustration in your life?

Possible causes of stress:

- Society – materialism, aspirations, relationships, home and church life, disconnection from nature and people.
- Occupational – demands, pressures, culture, time restraints, lack of resources.
- Biology – women respond to stress in different ways than men. Men tend to depersonalize and withdraw, and women become emotionally exhausted (Bermejo & Prieto, 2014) and release more cortisol (stress hormones) than men.
- Lifestyle – busy all the time. Little to no time for yourself or constructive reflection.
- Life changes – positive or negative (death, marriage, moving, money, holidays, lifestyle change, changes related to seasons of life).
- Psychology – negative outlook, internal conflicts, personality types—type A personalities experience more stress than type B (Blazer & MDCPS, 2010).

Identify your stress triggers and circle the areas below that are a source of stress for you.

- Social life
- Spiritual life
- Finances
- Employment
- Health and Fitness
- Family life
- Personal development/Purpose
- Environment
- Mental well-being
- Dreams/Goals/Aspirations

How often do you have each type of stress?
- Daily
- Weekly
- Monthly
- Never

Are you managing your stress well?
- Yes
- No

Has your stress level changed in the past year? If so, how?
- Decreased
- Increased
- Remained the same
- Fluctuated

Out of the above areas (i.e., social life, spiritual, financial, employment, health, and family, etc.) which stress triggers do you have? In what areas are you managing stress well and in what areas do you need to make changes?

Phases of Response

According to Dr. Hans Selye, our bodies go through a three-stage "stress response" (Selye, 2013). The responses are as follows:

Stage 1: Alarm Phase- fight or flight response
Your body makes the stress hormone cortisol and you will feel alert.

Stage 2: Resistance Phase
You will begin to feel the effects of lethargy, and your body starts taking away sex hormones and other hormones to produce more stress hormones.

Stage 3: Exhaustion Phase/Burnout Phase
Quality of life begins to diminish in this phase. Your body begins to struggle to produce the needed hormones to combat the stressors. Hormone levels become low and effect many bodily functions and daily living. You may become sick and lose interest in sex and other activities you once enjoyed. Burnout is evident during this phase.

- What phase do you most relate to at this point in time?
- Alarm Phase, Resistance Phase, or Exhaustion Phase/Burnout Phase
- If you are in the burnout phase, what degree of burnout are you experiencing?
  Low, moderate, or high?

Responses to Stress

According to the National Center for Education Statistics, 77 percent of teachers are female. Therefore, I will address female responses to stress. A women's health report, was released and shared by a local radio station reporting what women do after a day of stress.

Women tended to:

1. Eat sweets
2. Spend time alone
3. Drink wine

A closer look at these responses to stress reveals they can lead to other issues.

1. Eating sweets can lead to weight gain, diabetes, and foggy brain, which effects concentration. Energy is needed to continue the work of an educator and running to the sugars will deplete energy. They give momentary energy, not sustainable energy.

2. Spending time alone is good. If left unchecked, it can lead to depression and isolation. Depression can lead to sleeping more, being distant from others, and becoming apathetic.

3. Drinking wine. Some doctors have prescribed this to teachers. This can lead to alcoholism and in turn cause many other problems. I know you have heard of teachers drinking on the job. In the news, broadcasts have appeared of a teacher who went to school drunk and lost certification. My question was, what led the teacher to that point?

Our choices for stress management must be aligned with healthy productive strategies to live a life we are satisfied with.

Negative Responses/Outcomes to Stress:

- Physically: e.g., over sleeping, drinking, drugs, muscles become tense, rapid heartbeat, holding breath, hypertension, weight gain, headaches, fatigue, lack of sleep
- Emotionally: e.g., anger, frustration, withdrawal, depression, moodiness, temperamental (yelling, crying often, physically aggressive, over reacting), obsessing over the problem, becoming helpless or too helpful
- Mental: e.g., forgetful, lack of focus, attitude, consuming thoughts, being critical of yourself or others, negative thinking/worrying
- Behavioral: e.g., nervous behaviors such as biting nails, stuttering, fidgeting, and appetite changes (indulgence in foods/sweets, avoiding eating and eating disorders), withdrawing/lack of communication, consuming drugs (prescribed or otherwise) or alcohol, gambling/frequent shopping, self-injuring, contemplating suicide to avoid the pain or situation, poor self-care, becoming passive (ignoring how you feel, having the victim mentality all the time, avoiding problems), staying busy to avoid experiencing your feelings

My typical response to stress was to consume mountains of chocolate. At the end of many school days you could find me with chocolate in my hand. Now instead of eating the chocolate, I use the replacement behaviors of exercise, walking, and deep breathing for my stress. At the end of the school day I hug my little ones because I missed them, and a side benefit is endorphins are released, which combat stress.

I also withdrew at high periods of stress. I now have replaced withdrawing with my love of writing and reflecting with words. Reading has also served me well. Out of my struggles with stress this book has been produced.

It is not uncommon for individuals to go to extremes when coping with stress, difficult people, or circumstances. I have read about the teacher who wanted to commit suicide, and I've lived near a community in which a teacher did commit suicide because of the stress and strains of life. We all cope differently with life. There is not a one size fits all way to handle life. We each are given a different plan, building materials, and tools in life. It is up to each of us to determine how to use these tools. We have the power to change course, obtain new tools to finish the project (our life), and make a positive mark on the world. There are places to go if you feel like your situation calls for desperate measures. There is nothing too hard for God to handle. There are people waiting to receive a call if you are in need. There are prayer lines and people of faith—some of who have struggled through the same things—waiting for you to reach out. Here are a few resources if you or someone else needs some encouragement and guidance on this journey.

- Crisis Text Line (24/7): Text Home to 741741

- Hopeline: (Call or text): 1-877-235-4525

- National Suicide Prevention Lifeline (24/7): 1-800-273-TALK (8255)

- Son Life Prayer Line: 1-225-768-7000

- TBN Prayer line: 1-714-731-1000

- CBN Crisis Hotline: 1-800-823-6053

Selecting a positive response instead of a negative response will get the plan rolling to reduce and combat stress.

Circle a few new responses to implement below that you feel will serve you in the near future.

Positive Responses that serve as Replacement Behaviors:

- Listen to your self-talk.
- Watch what you focus on.
- Find ways to laugh more.
- Meditate throughout the day for a stress buster.
- Take time to quiet your mind and body.
- Take a brain break.
- Stop what you are doing throughout the day and change activities for a few minutes.
- Help someone else who is hurting or in need.
- Take a break when you feel aggravated or frustrated.
- Do something you enjoy. Have some good fun.
- Take the day of rest God created to actually rest.
- Make a list of the things you like about the job and read it daily.
- Build a good social support network.
- Have healthy relationships with others.
- Talk to others to reduce cortisol.
- Keep a stress diary for a week.*
- Simplify your daily routines.
- Learn a breathing technique that will work anywhere.
- Learn about your responses to stress and about stress in general.
- Learn to say NO.
- Reduce the stress at work: manage assignments and work, create systems that reduce the amount of clutter that collects, write a to do list, stretch, take breathing breaks.

- Eat healthy foods.
- Avoid caffeine and sugar.
- Avoid information overload.
- Assess other areas in your life that may feel out of control and start by making small changes.
- Drink daily allotment of water.
- Exercise– yoga, Pilates, pyro, swimming, biking, hiking, etc.
- Indulge in nature– spend time outside near water and trees.
- Take up a hobby you enjoy.
- Go to the spa; get a massage.
- Lighten up by thinking about the positive, instead of the negative.
- Do not respond emotionally to every stressor.
- Pray, pray, pray.

Determine what works best for you. Once you have mastered and made some of these a part of your routine, add another, and so on.

*Stress mindfulness or stress diary:
Become mindful of your stress levels and record details or keep a mental note of stressful situations for a week. Look for patterns. Are there any patterns with time, people, or certain events? Can you change any part of the situation or interaction to be less stressful?

I became more mindful of the times I felt stressed and aggravated. Right before I pulled into my home each day I felt a high level of stress. I had left a draining job only to start my next work load. Noticing this allowed me the opportunity to find a new response. I discovered that just a few minutes in the car before getting out allowed me to choose my attitude when I walked through the door, and it afforded me the time to make a mental list of the duties and priorities of the evening.

I also recognized that being around a certain personality type brought me anxiety. I had the ability to change this, and therefore I started spending more time with people who shared the same values. These slight changes made all the difference to my daily satisfaction level.

Now, it is your turn to identify ways to build resiliency and coping skills for your daily stressors.

- Are your coping skills positive or negative responses to life stressors?
- What do you currently do to alleviate stress?
- What replacement behaviors will serve you with the stressors in your life?
- What other coping skills can you adopt in your daily life?
- When faced with stressors, how will you respond to avoid adding to the stress level?
- Do you recognize any stress responses that are occurring? If so, which ones?
- What are your stress response patterns?

Recognize the coping patterns. Once you have identified your negative responses, you can find a replacement behavior that will work for you.

You may have to try a few things before finding your sweet spot. If your response tactic for coping creates other problems in your life it is likely negative in nature. Finding the good in the situation and thinking on these things is a start to building a wall to defeat the stress of life.

Consider some of the management techniques and skills discussed in the following chapter to prepare your stress reduction plan.

18

MANAGEMENT TECHNIQUES

Management Skill I–Breathing

Every time I use to read something about stress I would just skip the part about breathing. However, one day I read the book *Conscious Calm* by Laura Maciuika, and the importance of breathing and how it was related to de-stressing became clear. We must know ourselves to realize what our stressors are and how we are responding to them. Slowing down and breathing assists with being in tune with what our bodies and minds are communicating. This technique aids in the management of the daily stress. There are many great videos about using breathing techniques correctly to become centered and focused on breathing to reduce stress. Try it out. There may be a lot of huffing and puffing, but if done right, it will pay back with dividends immeasurable.

Management Skill II–Stretching & Exercise

Stretching is good for the body and takes the focus off the thing that is stressing you. Exercising releases endorphins (a group of hormones) that combat the stress hormone cortisol and produce euphoric feelings (Harvard Health, 2011). Stretching and exercising can be done in any location. The endorphins released during exercise aid in the prevention and reduction of life stressors. Stretching exercises range from low impact chair stretches you can do in the classroom to more complex yoga moves.

Here is a simple routine for a quick stress relief:

- Back stretch: Sit in a chair and lean forward for ten seconds, then lean backwards stretching arms as high as you can go.
- Seated spinal twist: Sit in the chair and turn to the left. Try to grab the back of the chair and hold for ten seconds, repeat doing this toward the right.
- Neck stretch: Sit in the chair and stretch the neck from side to side, holding each stretch for ten seconds, slowly release and stretch toward the opposite side.
- Leg stretch: Sit in the chair and extend the leg out with the heel on the floor, hold for thirty seconds, repeat with the opposite leg.
- Leg hug: Sit in the chair, pull your knees toward your chest with your feet in the chair, wrap your arms around your legs, and hold for thirty seconds.

There are several others you can try, and you can customize a quick stretch. A brisk walk is always great. If you can walk around the school once or to the other side for a quick five-minute exercise this may provide the stress reduction you need.

The article with visuals, "Stretches to do at Work Every Day," (deskercise) found on Healthline.com is a great source with a visual for each stretch that lasts from one to three seconds. A detailed list of the steps to perform the stretch are included under the virtual stretch.

Management Skill III–Sound

Sound is a driving force and it can stop stress in its tracks. Many stress reduction plans add music for relaxing or mood boosting to assist in managing stress. Soothing sounds and singing will boost the mood and provide energy. Whether we make a joyful noise by singing and humming or listening to sounds from nature, sounds can aid in combating stress. There are several apps for relaxing music and sounds. You can get into nature and enjoy the sounds and aesthetics. Find a local prayer garden or viewing garden and take a walk. Eliminating all sound is a stress buster. Frequent the beach or river to experience the healing powers of water. Listen to the waves crashing against the shore or the tide rolling away. The list is limitless. Find what you enjoy and add it to your plan.

Management Skill IV–Meditation, Not Medication

I sat in a meeting with educators and listened as they discussed the best medication to take for anxiety and stress. They shared the latest and greatest. One educator noted that she tried a prescription anxiety pill and it did not work. Then she proceeded to ask what would work for her anxiety. Another educator stated that all her friends were taking another type of prescription anxiety medication. I was in shock. My mouth hit the floor when I realized that over half the ladies in the meeting were on medication for anxiety related issues. Medication is a quick fix but often comes with side effects in the long term.

Meditation, the act of thinking on a specific thing, is an art that can save our mental and emotional health in ways medication cannot. Meditate on the good things and have a grateful heart for all that is right in your life. It could always be worse. If you must, get away and have a spa day or a day to yourself; it will do wonders for your well-being. "Finally, brethren, whatsoever things are true, whatsoever things are honest, whatsoever things are just, whatsoever things are pure, whatsoever things are lovely, whatsoever things are of good report; if there be any virtue, and if there be any praise, think on these things" (Phil. 4:8). Catching your thought patterns and changing them to think on good things can be a challenge. The more you practice this skill the better you will get at it. Meditate on a verse or virtuous saying to drive back stress and anxiety.

Management Skill V–Sweet Moments/Encouragement Folder

Recognition, awards, and accolades can add some momentary joy to the school year. These moments pass with time and the joy can fade with the memory. I was named Teacher of the Year the school year after my worst year ever. This sweet victory did not take away the frustrations and hardships of teaching. The wounds and pain were still fresh from the previous year, but my outlook was still positive, and I remained steadfast that I would make it through this school year, too.

The application process for Teacher of the Year requires you to obtain three letters of support. Upon receiving one of the truly personalized letters, I found an extra nugget to spur the school year on. The encouragement and positive notations in the letter were so uplifting. It helped me see the good I was doing and the progress I made even when it felt like I did not make any. I have an encouragement folder, and the folder contains letters from students, drawings, pictures, and so on. These types of things keep me going when I am down, frustrated, tired, and burnt out. I even have little notes in there from my own children and encouraging e-mails from co-workers. Creating your own encouragement file to save the sweet notes and pictures will give you encouragement, too. Encourage someone else in the profession with a kind word or uplifting message. Share with others how you were encouraged in keeping the sweet tokens of affection. I have even kept flowers and rocks to remind me that this is worth doing even on my hardest days.

Keep a gratitude journal or sweet moments journal to record the happy times. It is easy to be pessimistic and find the trouble in situations. It takes concerted effort to find the good and look for the joy even when we have sorrows and frustrations. However, this practice will create a happier life and it will shine through in all you do.

Management Skill VI–Share Your Situation with Others of Faith

Let someone else share the load. Share the situation you face with a believer. We stand together. You do not have to go the journey alone. In making others aware, they know what to pray for and how to lift your name up to the Lord. Exercise wisdom when deciding whom to share with. If you choose Negativity Nancy to talk with, you will fall deeper into despair. Surround yourself with those who will lift you up, pray for you, and encourage you. "A threefold cord is not quickly broken" (Eccles. 4:12) and where one can put a thousand to flight, two can put 10,000 to flight (Deut. 32:30). There is power in numbers, and when we bind together, yokes are broken. Joining a small group of believers in prayer and studying the Word will strengthen you.

Management Skill VII–Stay Fixed on the Lord, Not Feelings:

Teachers report many things. Here are a few:

One teacher reported, "I feel like I suck as a teacher!" She did not suck...she was just not able to be as effective as she wanted or preferred to be. This comes in part from overwhelming demands and not being trained to deal with the large demands that can be placed on you in a nano second. Being stretched thin is an understatement.

Another teacher said, "I don't even know why I came today!" There were so many interruptions she felt like she was accomplishing nothing of true value. Add burnout to the mix of a crazy day and you may be thinking the same thoughts.

Another teacher's comments included feeling like no one cared during her hardship year. She said, "It seems like it is never enough. They keep adding more to our loads." She felt like she could not carry the load. Some teachers feel as though others think they are not doing enough or their job load is little. So other assignments may be added to your load due to this.

A frustrated teacher shared that she does not feel like she is doing any good in any one area. She is pulled thin. She wears several job hats. She is not able to focus her days because the assignments and deadlines are too many.

One teacher shares in the small school district where she is employed, two teachers walked out before the end of the first quarter. The school is a tough school. The load was heavy and the demands too much. Therefore, the teachers left the profession.

Most of the comments were all based on feelings. Feelings are an important part of who we are; however, they cannot be what rules or leads us. Do what is right. God is a God of justice and righteousness. If you do your work as unto the Lord, he will reward you openly (Col. 3:23–24). It may not look like anything is happening. It may even appear that things are working against you. Do not despair; he is in the midst arranging all things for your good (Rom. 8:28). Remember, no matter how you feel or what the situation looks like stay focused on the Lord. Pray about how you feel and ask God to help you be proactive instead of reactive. He is a way maker and when he makes a way it is a blessing.

Management Skill VIII–Take Care of Yourself

This seems like an easy task, yet so many do not take care of themselves. When we are stressed out and tired we tend to focus on the feelings we are experiencing and how we need more rest. The rest seldom comes because our minds are racing about the difficult tasks at hand and the long list awaiting us tomorrow. We wake in the middle of the night thinking about it, whatever your *it* is. We tend to not eat right and skip out on the exercise. We often find complaining has become our best friend and that our best friend is tired of hearing us complain. It is a vicious cycle that is exacerbated by the approach we take in handling our own well-being. We cannot set our well-being aside to meet the demands of a profession that needs us to be on the top of our game to give our best to the students and co-workers. To sum up Luke 12:22–31, take care of your spiritual life and the other things you need will come. The Lord has sent us to serve and not be served. To serve well you must take care of yourself. If you have health related issues take care of them. Do not put them aside or wait. You will be around much longer for your loved ones and can work towards fulfilling your destiny if you care for yourself.

Ways to care for yourself:

- Eat right
- Meditate/Pray
- Take a breathing break
- Think positive thoughts
- Seek help if needed (We cannot do it all.)
- Remember you are most effective when you are taking care of yourself
- Join a support group or Teacher Life Group
- Exercise or take a walk

- Find a quiet place for a few minutes and think about nothing
- Address any health issues with fervency

Management Skill IX–Operable Systems

Create systems that work for you. Being unorganized and having mountains of inoperable systems will cause distress. Create systems that keep you organized. Search and strive for ways to stay organized. Here is what I use to stay organized:

Master List:
A list of all the to dos I have on my radar. I list them out and add them to my weekly schedule as I determine necessary.

Full Year Outlook:
This is where I keep track of specifics that need to be done in the future. This information can also be added to the side of your master calendar for upcoming events or to dos.

Master Calendar/Weekly Planning:
My calendar with meetings, appointments, and so on. This can be paper or digital. This is where the master list, master calendar, and the full year outlook come together. I carve out time to plan the next week and organize my weekly calendar.

Being organized relieves stress and creates confidence that you can be successful on the job. For many, the time management system we have does not work well. Sticky notes are great. However, after the sticky notes pile up and you re-write the information on them several times over, you realize that a new system needs to be implemented. I learned that combining personal and professional on one calendar also assists in staying organized and simplifying things. Keep the planner in a place that allows you to see it daily. An expert shared a tip to keep it by the bathroom sink or on your pillow. You will see this daily when you get ready or in the evening before bed to prepare for the next day.

There are many great books on time management and organization. Choose two or three from a local library or book store to read. Search for tools and systems that will work with your personality. Implement two to three of the ideas. Review the system that you chose and tweak it if necessary. A system will give you organization that will support your everyday activities.

When organizing your life, keep in mind to:

- Prioritize and schedule life.
- Commit to the changes you decide to make.
- Work wisely, assess students wisely, etc.
- Have a clearly set personal boundary—give only a certain amount of your personal time to any job-related activities. Limit the time you spend on work related activities at home so it does not consume too much time and energy from your day.

Management Skill X–Plan Ahead

There are years that summer plans need to be simplified. Many educators pack the summer with workshops, conferences, make and take, traveling, and some even work. If you have had a tough year and feel very burned out, it is time to take heed and listen to what your body, mind, and spirit need. You need rejuvenation. Filling the summer with busy activities may only add fuel to the fire. Limit the number of extra activities that you undertake in the summer and on breaks, too. You need it! The next group of students you work with deserve you to be at your best, and you cannot give it your all when you are working in burnout mode. Begin to choose approaches to stress reduction that are going to fit into your life style and how you approach life.

Management Skill XI–Remember to Teach

Recall the acronym TEACH:

T–take a deep breath
E–encourage yourself
A–act in faith
C–choose to be your best and control negative thoughts
H–Hold tight to the Lord's promises

19

DETERMINE YOUR WHY

If you feel like you cannot make it another year in education or another day, there are questions to ask yourself to determine your why, the reason why you teach.

- What drives me to teach?
- What are my motives for being a teacher?
- Am I following what has heart and meaning for me?
- Am I being true to myself?
- Why am I in this profession? Is it to get a paycheck or to make a difference in others' lives? Maybe it is for the days off and the benefits?

Whatever your reason is you will need to soul search and determine your why. This "why" will drive you to stay if the why is for the right reasons. Having a clear why will enable you to make educated decisions about your future and the future of the students you work with. Education is about the students and the future of our whole society. Being strong enough to finish the course, at least to the end of the year, for the students shows commitment. Even if the job is tough, the students need you. I posted a quote in my classroom, commitment is staying when the feeling we started out with fades.

There are some conditions to staying:

If your health or safety is in danger you need to address that as the priority. This includes mental health, too. There are some paraprofessionals and teachers who have had nervous breakdowns or strokes. Why do we let it get to this point?

At this time, the educational system does not have a system set up for this type of situation, so we are responsible, even if the nervous breakdown or stroke came from the stress of the job. Be proactive. If you are not in good health, can you give your best to the students and should you put your own life on the line? Seek professional medical advice about your situation and health history to make decisions that are best for you. If your health warrants, check into approved stress leave from employment. Each district/area has different guidelines. Therefore, check into the stipulations for medical leave due to stress related illness.

20

TEACHERS NEED OPTIONS

Even after my battle was long over I felt stuck in my job. I felt like there was no way out. I was boxed in by needing a certain salary to survive and felt trapped by the circumstances that surrounded my employment. One being my own fear to embrace any change in my job, and the other being the fact that I did not have any other recent experience except teaching.

After fasting and praying to the Lord about another option, he answered. I went on a trip to a food fest. During this trip, I was walking around searching for any clue or hint at some other avenue to seek for employment that would be the right fit. One booth caught my attention. It was a booth an immigration lawyer had set up. I walked up to see the questions they had in large bold print, challenging Americans to answer questions immigrants answer to gain citizenship into America. I spoke with the lady who stood behind the booth. She was a teacher, like me. She taught in another state. However, when she moved to a new state she could not find a job. She then sought out other options. She discovered that you can study in different academic areas and take a Praxis test in that certain subject area. Once you pass the test you can add certification onto your teaching certificate. She shared that she passed in other areas and added the certifications onto her certificate. She loved teaching the new subject areas. I told her about the prayer I lifted up right before I went into the food fest. She said, "You know if the lawyer would have been here I would not have had this conversation with you." She confirmed she knew it was the Lord's answer to my prayer.

Each state has different requirements. However, we do have other options and we don't have to feel trapped or boxed into one position. For more information in this area look up Certification by Test for your state. There will be opened and closed doors along life's journey. "The steps of a good man are ordered by the LORD" (Ps. 37:23) and he will open the right doors. We just have to knock.

If you have grown bored or feel complacent with your teaching job, National Teacher Board Certification may be a choice to get you out of a rut. This certification allows for growth where you are and to go deeper into making meaningful impacts for your students. Many educators have noted this process is the most rewarding professional experience and well worth the time. There are about forty states that compensate for this extra certification. For more details check out this process online www.nbpts.org or for additional information, contact the National Board for Professional Teaching Standards at (800) 22-TEACH.

21

TRANSITIONS

I frequently found myself pondering what I wanted to do with my life. The stresses and strains of teaching were heavy. I longed to transition into another area of daily work. I thought, if you spend a majority of your time at work, it should be enjoyable. Most educators enjoy the teaching part of the job. It is the extra that comes along with the job that ends up not being so enjoyable. Each job has unenjoyable parts, but when the stresses are so numerous, it makes the enjoyable part not so enjoyable. What makes us stay?

This can be attributed to many things:

- Not sure what else you want to do as a career
- Financial obligations that keep you locked in
- The fear of change and the unknown
- The fact that many love the schedule so we can be with our own children or pursue other interests
- The hope and desire that we are making a difference
- The fact that we spend a lot of money, time, and energy to gain a degree we no longer want to use

If we find that we truly need to make a career change, we can make it through the school year by focusing on the positive aspects and by creating a plan to transition into another career.

Transitions take time. The first place to start out is to get to know you. Make a list of the things you want and do not want out of your next career or job venture. What lifestyle do you want to live on a daily basis? Become clear about your wants and needs in life. Change the things you can to make them better or workable for you and your situation. Embrace the things you have no control over and move on. Each vocation has its pros and cons. Making the right decisions will drive you to make the right moves in your future.

22

CAREER REFLECTION

Know if you are in the right culture for your personality. Each of us has a different personality and we blend well with some and not so well with others. If a school culture is toxic and affects you negatively, you may need to look into employment in another school. However, do your homework and determine if the culture you are contemplating moving into is a good fit. You can never completely avoid difficult people.

If the group is tainted with negative attitudes, consistent complaining, and unprofessionalism it may be time to rethink your placement. There are times we are in a place for a reason, to make a positive impact. God may be using you to be the light that shines into a specific school for the staff and students. Another relevant question to consider is am I in a culture that matches my beliefs and morals? If you are not aligned to your own values, then satisfaction could wane. Maybe a change of schools or job assignment will benefit you.

If you are unsure of what direction or route to take, ask yourself pertinent questions that allow you to reflect deeply:

- What are you willing to pay for the paycheck?
- Are you willing to be stressed to the level you are?
- Are you willing to give the time and effort needed?
- Are you willing to make the sacrifices you make?

- What changes should be made?
- How can you find balance in your daily life in this career?
- What is the root cause of dissatisfaction with the current job and/or profession?
- Is this work meaningful to you?
- Do you feel like you are making a positive impact or a difference in the world?
- Are you growing as an individual on and off the job?
- What specific areas do you dislike? What can you do to change this?
- Are you taking care of yourself?
- What is important for you right now?
- What do you want? Use the 1-1-1 rule. Where do you want to be in 1 month, 1 year, and 1 decade?
- What step/s can you take next?
- How can you simplify life? (Ex: live closer to job, coordinate schedules) Determine what you need to do to simplify your job while remaining effective.

Determine what you want and what you don't.

Here is an example:

Want:
- Low stress
- Flexibility with time
- Decent Pay
- Stable Career

Do not want:
- Overly demanding job
- Extreme amounts of paperwork while juggling other heavy work loads
- Negative culture to work in for long periods of time

If you want or feel led to change careers, there are several steps to take. Prayerfully create a list of the job ventures or career areas you are interested in. Then research these jobs online, interview others who are already serving in the area of interest, and possibly volunteer to see if this is the direction you plan to head. There may be an area in education that you are better suited for. You may have always wanted to start a business. Making prayer a part of your search will lead you to the answer.

Then determine the path you want to head down. This will take time, because you want to make sure your next move is the right one for you and your situation. There are many things to take into consideration for your next career decision. You may want to move into another area in the education field or start completely over. The options are vast. You may need to pay off debt and downsize the home or car because your dream job does not pay what you currently need to survive. Therefore, it is crucial to create a transition plan. Each individual's plan will be unique to his or her life and desires. There is no one size fits all solution.

There may be times it feels like you will not ever get the job you desire. Maybe you think, I don't know the right person to get the job. Recall that you know the Lord above and no man can close any door the Lord opens (Rev. 3:8) and no one can open any door the Lord shuts. It is in his timing and placement when the right door will open for you. Sometimes we have to wait and the waiting room is a tough place to be. If you keep the Lord's ways you will inherit the land (Ps. 37:34). Don't give up. Keep knocking on doors for opportunities.

Use the following example transition tool to create a plan for the next step you desire to take in life.

Career Transition Plan

Purpose: To create a "PLAN" for career transition to keep me on track.
Goal: 1. To determine what career I would like to move into. 2. Take the steps to move into that career.

Action Steps What Will Be Done?	Responsibilities Who Will Do It?	Timeline By When? (Day/Month)	Things to Do	Potential Barriers A. What? B. How?	Other Plans
Step 1: Determine which career that I would like to transition into.	Crystal B	Projected Date	1. Volunteer to work at places in the area of possible interest. 2. Interview others in that job career. 3. Pray for direction. 4. Research jobs and opportunities.	A. B.	
Step 2: Continue your planning in this manner.				A. B.	

Evidence of Success: *(How will you know that you are making progress? What are your benchmarks? A clear career direction will be determined and the steps will be put in place and taken.*
Evaluation Process: *(How will you determine that your goal has been reached? What are your measures? Goal will be reached when a successful career move has been made.*

23

DO WHAT YOU CAN

We can only do so much in a day. As educators, we must realize we are human.

Hold yourself to realistic expectations and recognize when you are being unrealistic. Do all things as unto the Lord and not unto man (Col. 3:17). Be pleasing in the Lord's eyes.

There are times of overwhelm. Dread may fill the day or the feeling of burnout may consume. In these times, "I will lift up mine eyes unto to the hills, from whence cometh my help. My help cometh from the LORD" (Ps. 121:1–2). I will rest in the Lord and keep my eyes fixed on him. I can make it through the school year, with the Lord on my mind and by my side. He "is a friend that sticketh closer than a brother" (Prov. 18:24). Though it may get rough and it seems like the enemy is coming "in like a flood, the Spirit of the LORD shall lift up a standard against him" (Isa. 59:19). I will trust in him. "He only is my rock and my salvation: he is my defense; I shall not be moved" (Ps. 62:6). "I can [make it through the school year] do all things through Christ which strengtheneth me" (Phil 4:13).

24

CHANGES ON THE HORIZION

We live in a technological world, yet in schools we have not made the advances that are necessary to yield the results desired in education. Technology can be an avenue for teachers to collaborate and share on a larger scale. How many teachers across the world made a lesson plan and prepared activities to teach the same skill as you?

We need to be connected. Teachers are often not connected due to time restraints. However, if educators were more connected we could save time by being open and sharing the resources we have. Some educators are great at this.

I have had the opportunity to work daily with several educators and over the course of many years I have found that some educators are willing to share ideas and materials and others seem to be afraid that if they share a resource it somehow makes them less than you or you are taking away from who they are as an educator. When I first went into education, I saw competition occurring frequently. I thought this was normal, so I did it. It is not normal, so I changed my approach! I began to share more and it brought me joy to be able to help others. A common vision is fundamental. Competition should not be the driving force in education. Teaching should encompass the common goal of educating students and making a difference in the lives of others. Being an agent of change will pave the way for reformation to take place. More cohesion in education will yield a crop of productivity.

25

I CAN AND I WILL MAKE IT THROUGH THE SCHOOL YEAR

You do not have to break under the pressure. You can be like a flexi ruler and bend, but not break. This season too shall pass, therefore, have patience. We usually associate patience with waiting. Patience is about how we respond in the waiting period or during the test. My test seemed to go on forever with no end in sight. I felt like a repeater in the same grade day after day. I longed to pass the test and move up to the next level. I had to realize what God wanted me to overcome. Through the test, God revealed things in my heart and has molded me to become a better person. Through each test God has drawn me closer to him.

Battles that bring you closer to God are blessings for you. Circumstances can and will change. God can change our circumstances in the blink of an eye. We have to stand the test. When you have done all you can do to stand, just stand. Stand in the truth, in the Word, and in faith (Eph. 6:13).

I have been like the waves in my battle. One second I am filled with faith and the next I am repeating to myself how I am tired of the pressure and the battle. Worrying does not change the situation or the circumstance. By worrying you cannot add one more cubit or change your stature (Matt. 6:27). Through it all I learned to wait patiently and that means not just waiting but how we wait and what kind of attitude we have while we wait on the Lord. It is not always easy waiting, but it is sure worth it. God always has something better in store for us than we would have picked for ourselves. "Wait, I say, on the LORD" (Ps. 27:14).

For those who do not have a relationship with the Lord or maybe you drifted away there is no better time than now to establish this relationship. God will never fail you nor leave you stranded. He will pick you up when you can go no further. He will speak peace and life into your situation. This relationship can begin today by speaking these words with a true heart:

Heavenly Father, I know I need a Savior and that I can do nothing without you. I have sinned and am sorry for the things I have done wrong in my life. Please forgive me for my sins. Thank you for Christ who paid the ultimate price for my sins. Help me, Lord, to learn to walk in your ways. In Jesus name I pray, amen.

A simple prayer like this allows God to infiltrate your life and begin to do a good work. This opens the door for the Lord to begin his work in your life. Find a good Bible-based church to draw strength from. The Word of God can be found in many places…read it daily, post it around the places you spend a lot of time, have it sent to your phone via text message, and so on. Be creative. It will provide strength to you and help you make it through the school year.

So many days I wanted to quit, to walk away, and throw my hands up in the middle of the school year. I thought, I cannot make it through this year. For reasons bigger than me and unknown to me, God brought me through this hardship to serve a purpose. I believe that purpose was to be a deliverer of the message that we *can* make it through the school year, we are conquerors (Rom. 8:37), and no weapon formed against us shall prosper (Isa. 54:17). If we cast our cares onto him (Ps. 55:22) and lay down our burdens, he will carry us (Isa. 46:4) through the school year.

After that long difficult year I had gained new mental and spiritual strength. I had overcome in the Lord. I still had some apprehension about returning the next year. I looked for other jobs and applied. However, it was not the Lord's will. God did not move when I wanted him to or how I wanted him to. He knows what we have need of before we even present our need to him (Matt. 6:8). He already knows our battle and he is working it out for our good. God sees the bigger picture. It was not about me, my situation, or how I was feeling. It was about what God wanted to do and his plan being fulfilled. The battle was won in the Lord! I made it through and you can too!

EPILOGUE

1. Meditate (think) on the good things. It is easy to find what is not going right or to focus on being overwhelmed or stressed. Instead, focus on doing your best and remember you are human and can only do so much. In the education setting, the work and requirements can pile up fast. You can find yourself in a place that is frustrating. You are doing all you can to stay afloat and the demands are weighing on you. This can lead to burnout if it is not handled in an effective manner. Remain focused and do what you can. You will accomplish more with this approach. Do not compare yourself to the next educator. Each of our battles is different. If your focus remains on your work and not the work of others you will be more successful. Help me, Lord, to focus on the right things.

2. Remain flexible and go with the flow. The work will pile up and continue to grow. Do the most important and time sensitive tasks first and then go back to the task you were focused on. Everything will not get done.

3. Don't feel stuck or alone when facing a hardship or a tough year and want to throw in the towel. God has a plan for you, and you have been placed in a specific location at a specific time to serve a greater purpose. God's promise in Isaiah is a truth to hold onto. "When thou passest through the waters, I will be with thee; and through the rivers, they shall not overflow thee: when thou walkest through the fire, thou shalt not be burned; neither shall the flame kindle upon thee" (Isa. 43:2).

4. Be thankful for all things. The Lord has taught me to be thankful or to extend gratitude to the Lord. This is contagious. Others around you will become more

thankful and the atmosphere will be one with peace and gratitude from those around you. This one change can be profound.

5. Teach from the heart.

6. Every dollar has a price tag. We pay a price for every decision we make. What price are you willing to pay? Think decisions through.

7. Survival mode is feeling like quitting or giving up. It is hard to see the positive in this frame of mind. Part of you stops caring like you once did. Remember the reason/s why you took this career path.

8. Pray for strength. When I asked for the Lord's help, my school day was better. Seek outside help if needed. Call on the name of Jesus. Recall the Serenity Prayer.

9. God will make the crooked road straight. When trouble comes, keep the faith. Think on the promises of God. Read Isaiah 40:4-5.

10. Ask yourself: Did you do what you could do? The poem "Broken Dreams" is a picture of how to trust God when we have done all we can do.

11. Handle the problem and do not let the problem handle you.

12. Learn from the experience: What is God teaching you or how is he molding you?

13. Locate a Bible verse or inspirational quote that gives you encouragement and strength. As teachers, we have the privilege to impact the lives of children from all walks of life. Some come to us from broken or dysfunctional

homes with many needs. We can rely and trust in God almighty to help us through each and every moment.

14. Long term stress can have negative effects on health. These vary from strokes, high blood pressure, obesity, heart disease, and diabetes. To win the war on stress, healthy responses and habits are necessary to form.

15. Have a made-up mind to know how you will wait for answers to prayer. Decide that you will wait expectantly and joyfully because your answer or breakthrough is just around the corner. (See Jer. 29:11)

16. Give your brain some free time to just rest. Sometimes we have to stop being busy getting it all done and address student needs that are not related to academics. We may need to address our own needs, too. Take the time to do this.

17. We do not know everything. Seek out assistance and the wisdom of others you trust. You do not know everyone's story and they do not know yours. Be a support system to others.

18. The hard times make you know what is working and what is not. We have a cross to bear. You grow more in difficult times. God will answer you. His grace is sufficient. He puts us in a place to use us and will line it all up. We may be in the wilderness so we can, like Joseph, feed our brothers and sisters. Use your experience for your testimony.

19. Never settle for less than God's best for your life. Our time is limited, so we need to live it to fulfil our purpose or destiny. Find your area of gifting and what you are passionate about. Pick and choose what area you need to focus on.

20. Let God have your dreams. He will work through you. We cannot be proud or boastful saying, look at me and how great I am. We need to look at God and say how great he is. He will use us as he will, so hold onto Jesus. Sometimes we want out of a situation or place, but it is just where God wants us to be.

21. If you are unhappy with areas of your life, take steps to change them. You have a choice to continue life as it is or change life as it is.

22. Team up with others. Find others that complement your strengths and weaknesses. Provide support to others. Encourage one another. When we look around we can find someone to help or a need to meet. Find meaning by adding value to others.

23. Remember this is bigger than we are, and we do not know what the Lord is doing behind the scenes. One teacher shared how tragedy was avoided in a student's life because of the impact the teacher made.

24. Recall you are not the only one Googling or Binging these words: burnout, stressed, culture, overloaded, politics, challenging students, bad boss, difficult situation, jobs, difficult people, dissatisfied with job, career change, and so on. You are not alone.

25. Focus on what you have control over in your life and circle of influence. You control your attitude and how you respond to the situation. Use mindfulness techniques. Focus on what you are doing and not on what others are doing.

26. "Fear thou not; for I am with thee; be not dismayed; for I am thy God: I will strengthen thee; yea, I will uphold thee with the right hand of my righteousness." (Isaiah 41:10).

27. Create a positive narrative to keep you going. Ignore negativity.

28. Avoid causing undue problems and stress. Use integrity and wisdom in all you do, even when posting on social media outlets. Use inversion to learn what not to do, learn from those who act inappropriately. Do not repeat their mistakes.

REFERENCES

Chapter 2

Poem, Broken Dreams, can be found at
http://epistle.us/inspiration/brokendreams.html

McNamara, Robert. (2017, June 14). Abraham Lincoln Quotations Everyone Should Know. Retrieved from https://thoughtco.com/abraham-lincoln-quotations-everyone-should-know-1773576

Chapter 11

    Goldring, R., Taie, S., and Riddles, M. (2014). Teacher Attrition and Mobility: Results From the 2012–13 Teacher Follow-up Survey (NCES 2014-077). U.S. Department of Education. Washington, DC: National Center for Education Statistics. Retrieved [September 6, 2017] from http://nces.ed.gov/pubsearch.

    Gray, L., and Taie, S. (2015). Public School Teacher Attrition and Mobility in the First Five Years: Results From the First Through Fifth Waves of the 2007–08 Beginning Teacher Longitudinal Study (NCES 2015-337). U.S. Department of Education. Washington, DC: National Center for Education Statistics. Retrieved [August 27, 2017] from http://nces.ed.gov/pubsearch.

    Hughes, A. L., Matt, J. J., & O'Reilly, F. L. (2015). Principal Support Is Imperative to the Retention of Teachers in Hard-to-Staff Schools. *Journal of Education and Training Studies*, *3*(1), 129-134.

Chapter 12

Baker, B. D., & Welner, K. G. (2010). Premature Celebrations: The Persistence of Inter-District Funding Disparities. *Education Policy Analysis Archives, 18*(9).

Chapter 15

Stress Effects. Retrieved September 04, 2017, from, American Institute of Stress, https://www.stress.org/stress-effects/

"Top Ten Most Stressful Jobs in America." Retrieved September 05, 2017, from http://abcnews.go.com/GMA/be_your_best/page/top-10-stressful-jobs-america-14355387

Chapter 16

Blazer, C., & Miami-Dade County Public Schools, R. S. (2010). Teacher Burnout. Information Capsule. Volume 1003.

"Top Ten Most Stressful Jobs in America." Retrieved September 05, 2017, from http://abcnews.go.com/GMA/be_your_best/page/top-10-stressful-jobs-america-14355387

Chapter 17

Greenberg, M. T., Brown J. L., Abenavoli, R.M. (2016). "Teacher Stress and Health Effects on Teachers, Students, and Schools." Edna Bennett Pierce Prevention Research Center, Pennsylvania State University.

Bermejo-Toro, L., & Prieto-Ursúa, M. (2014). "Absenteeism, Burnout and Symptomatology of Teacher Stress: Sex Differences." *International Journal of Educational Psychology*, *3*(2), 175-201.

Goldring, R., Taie, S., and Riddles, M. (2014). Teacher Attrition and Mobility: Results From the 2012–13 Teacher Follow-up Survey (NCES 2014-077). U.S. Department of Education. Washington, DC: National Center for Education Statistics. Retrieved [August 27, 2017] from http://nces.ed.gov/pubsearch.

Taie, S. & Goldring , R (2017). Characteristics of Public Elementary and Secondary School Teachers in the United States: Results from the 2015-16 National Teacher and Principal Survey First Look (NCES 2017-072). U.S. Department of Education. Washington D.C.: National Center for Education Statistics. Retrieved [August 27, 2017] from https://nces.ed.gov/pubsearch/pubsinfo.asp?pubid=201707 2.

Selye, H. (2013). *Stress in health and disease*. Butterworth-Heinemann.

Chapter 18

Publications, H. H. (n.d.). Exercising to relax. Retrieved September 16, 2017, from https://www.health.harvard.edu/staying-healthy/exercising-to-relax

www.ingramcontent.com/pod-product-compliance
Lightning Source LLC
Chambersburg PA
CBHW070521030426
42337CB00016B/2047